WALK!
IN
ASHDOWN F....

Christine Baldwin

S.B. Publications

First published in 2002 by S. B. Publications
19 Grove Road, Seaford, East Sussex BN25 1TP
Tel: 01323 893498

ISBN 1 85770 239 5

Designed and Typeset by EH Graphics (01273) 515527
Printed by Page Turn Limited (01273) 821500

Front cover photo: Looking across Wren's Warren
Back cover photo: Area in valley near Airman's Grave
Title page photo: Pooh (sticks) Bridge.

Photographs by Christine Baldwin

CONTENTS

The Little Hiker series

'The Little Hiker'.

An original woodcarving by Rita Keatley
Illustrated by Rita Keatley

ACKNOWLEDGMENTS

I would like to thank Rita for accompanying me on walks in Ashdown Forest,
also for her contribution of the Little Hiker.

Note that the landscape, around walks 2, 3,5 and possibly others, may have changed
due to coppicing, to encourage new growth and wildlife to flourish.

INTRODUCTION

Ashdown Forest lies between Forest Row and Uckfield and consists of 6,400 acres of woodland and heathland just waiting to be explored.

Ashdown Forest (or Lancaster Great Park) has its origins dating from 1372 and was considered an ideal area for hunting by the aristocracy.

By the sixteenth century, iron ore and charcoal burning were the main source of industry causing a great deal of conflict between local people for the wood. To this day iron ore deposits still colour the streams, and iron slag can be found in sunken hollows.

In 1693 a decree gave the Commoners (people who farmed the land) half the land. Feuding was rife, with conflicting interests of use lasting right up to 1885.

An Act of Parliament gave Commoners certain rights but it was not until 1974 that the public were given right of access over the whole forest.

Heathland covers over half of the forest area, which in turn supports wildlife, cattle, sheep and deer. Certain areas are prolific with bracken, heather, sedge grass, along with mosses. Other areas have Cotton-grass, Ling heather, European and Dwarf gorses. In the wet heathland areas Bog Cotton, Purple Moor grass, Cross-leaved Heather and Bog Asphodel can be seen. Woodland areas have Scots Pine, Birch, Oak, along with worked Chestnut, Alder, and Hazel trees.

Look out for squirrels, hedgehogs, rabbits, foxes and badgers all over the forest, along with many species of birds, insects, and even the odd reptile. Sheep are often seen wandering freely, enhancing the feeling of open countryside. The deer are more elusive, often only leaving tracks or an antler, where they rested.

In all seasons the forest has something to offer the visitor. Springtime brings forth new life, young can be seen or heard and new growth appears underfoot in the woods, which endorses the feeling of a new year.

In the summer carpets of blue and purple, intertwined with greens and yellows cover the valleys and open spaces. The views are captivating by their colours.

Autumn brings on the shades of browns and reds as the trees bear their fruit, then start to lose their leaves, undergrowth dies back till the following spring and wildlife look for their winter homes. Various types of fungi add a new dimension of colour to the forest floor. Winter brings out a bareness of open wilderness, broken only by the evergreens standing tall. Streams are high and animal tracks can be seen in the mud and on frosty mornings.

This is an area for a day out or a holiday, a walk, hike, or just a stroll. Steeped in history, with the added attraction of a famous bear and his friends, Ashdown Forest has plenty to offer everyone.

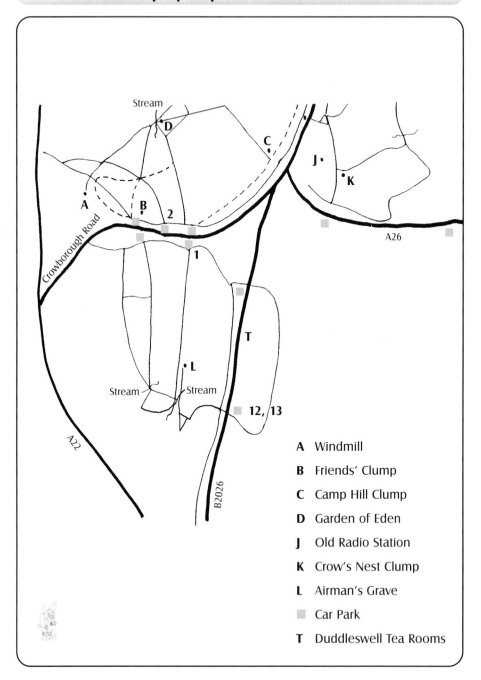

A   Windmill

B   Friends' Clump

C   Camp Hill Clump

D   Garden of Eden

J   Old Radio Station

K   Crow's Nest Clump

L   Airman's Grave

   Car Park

T   Duddleswell Tea Rooms

WALKS 3, 4, 5, 6, 10, 11, 14, 15, 16 STARTING POINT

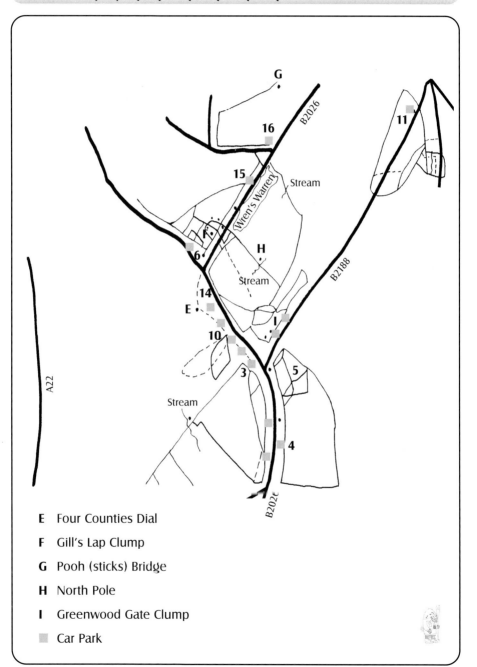

E   Four Counties Dial

F   Gill's Lap Clump

G   Pooh (sticks) Bridge

H   North Pole

I   Greenwood Gate Clump

▨   Car Park

WALKS 9, 17, 20, 22, 23 STARTING POINT

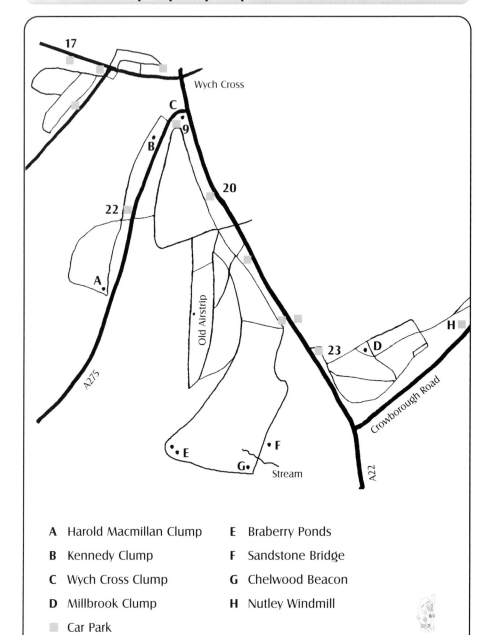

A Harold Macmillan Clump

B Kennedy Clump

C Wych Cross Clump

D Millbrook Clump

◼ Car Park

E Braberry Ponds

F Sandstone Bridge

G Chelwood Beacon

H Nutley Windmill

WALKS 7, 8, 18, 19, 21 STARTING POINT

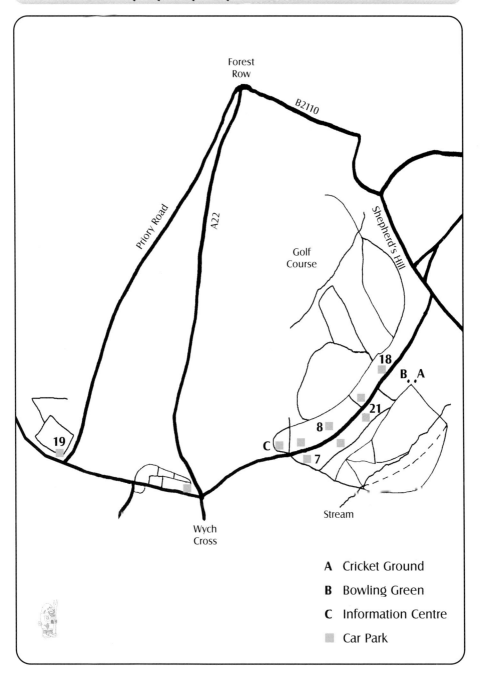

Forest Row

B2110

Priory Road

A22

Shepherd's Hill

Golf Course

18

B **A**

21

8

C

7

19

Wych Cross

Stream

A Cricket Ground

B Bowling Green

C Information Centre

■ Car Park

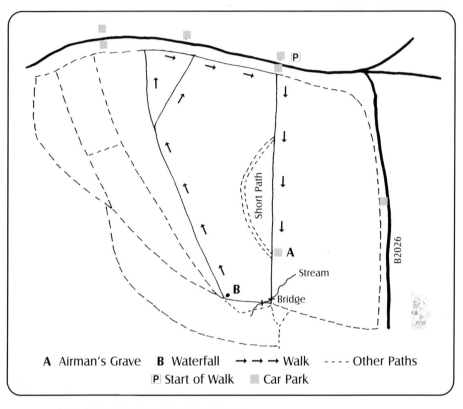

A Airman's Grave   **B** Waterfall   → → → Walk   - - - - Other Paths
P Start of Walk   ▨ Car Park

Access/Parking:	Hollies car park (page 6)
Map reference:	EX 135. 463287
Distance:	4mls (Short walk 1ml)
Time:	2hrs (Short walk ³/₄ - 1hr)
Terrain:	Steep uphill climb, on short and long walk. Muddy when wet. Uneven paths. This walk can be strenuous, but well worth it.
Refreshments:	Nutley village ¹/₂ml.

Points of interest

A. Airman's Grave.

Airman's Grave is a monument to the occupants of a Wellington bomber of 142 Squadron during World War II. It was first a single wooden cross, with a wooden fence surrounding, placed by the mother of one of the pilots. In 1972 the present plaque and stone wall were erected with the help of the local Conservators. Remembrance Sunday is a special day, with locals and public laying poppies. A well known area in Ashdown. Try not to miss it.

B. Waterfall.

Route directions

From the car park head downhill on the main path, keeping to the right hand side of parked cars.

Steep hill down.

The path is worn away by time and feet with uneven ground.

Views as you look across the valley are spectacular.

Airman's Grave (A) is near the bottom of hill.

From this point there are two walks.

To the right of the grave a path, through bracken and heather, goes across the valley and back up the hill.

Carry on down the hill to the stream.

Cross over the stream. Bear left.

Climb small slope. Path comes out on to a flat path with bracken/heather each side.

Path follows the stream. Also passing through bog areas with path up/down.

Coming to the waterfall (B) the path drops down steeply.

Cross over the waterfall.

Now climb back up on a well-trodden path, with growth of bracken often at body height.

A slow climb allows you to hear and often see a variety of wildlife. Look out over the valley. Beautiful scenery is visible in all directions.

The path brings you on to a wide grass horse track path.

Turn right.

Walk along the path to the car park.

Airman's Grave

WALK 2 Two Clumps and a Windmill

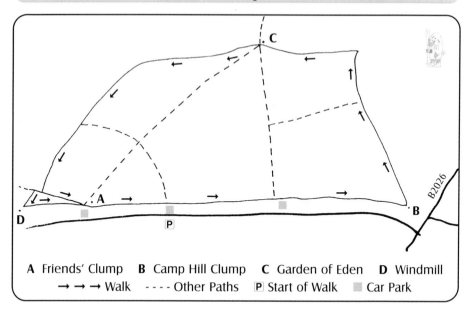

A Friends' Clump **B** Camp Hill Clump **C** Garden of Eden **D** Windmill
→ → → Walk   - - - - Other Paths   P Start of Walk   ▨ Car Park

Access/Parking:	Box car park (page 6)
Map reference:	EX 135. 460288
Distance:	3mls (Short walk 1½mls)
Time:	1½ - 2hrs (Short walk 1hr)
Terrain:	Steep hills. Wide paths. Eroded in some parts. Muddy when wet. This walk can start from Friends'/Ellisons Pond car parks. Well worth the hills.
Refreshments:	Nutley village ½ml.

Points of interest

A. Friends' Clump.
Friends' Clump was planted in 1973 - the 'Year of the Tree' - by the Friends of Ashdown Forest.

B. Camp Hill Clump.
Camp Hill Clump was planted in 1825 as a landscape feature. The name originates from the successive military camps in the area since the Middle ages.

C. Garden of Eden.

D. Nutley Windmill. Open on the last Sunday of each month from June/September only, from 2.30 - 5.30pm.

Route directions

From Box car park turn right. Sand path takes you along to Ellisons Pond.
Walking past first pond, path leads uphill, with a second pond on the right. Steep climb.
Once at the top the view is panoramic. This area is Camp Hill Clump (B).
From Camp Hill Clump (B) walk downhill, looking over fields in the distance. At the

second junction downhill, turn left. Wide muddy path takes you down into the Garden of Eden (C)

Short walk
From the Garden of Eden (C) carry on up the hill in front of you. Steep climb. Clump of Scots Pine trees in view at the top. This area is Friends' Clump (A). Turn left at top. Path goes round to the car park.

Long walk
From Garden of Eden (C) bear right up the slope. Bear to the right out on to a flat path.
On your right are woods of Scots Pine, Oak and Silver Birch. On the

Nutley Windmill

left fields of heather abound. Come to crossroads. Carry straight on. Now path starts to climb up. Passing more woods on right, path comes out on to wide grass path.
For Windmill turn right.
200yds turn left.
Go up grass path, through a gate to the windmill.
With the windmill behind you head towards a cottage on your right. Pass through a gate, and along to the path. Bench to be found at junction with main path.
At junction with bench, stop and take in the view. For miles in all directions you will see fantastic scenery.
Path carries on uphill, out on to flat.
Now Friends' Clump (A) is in view. Still on the flat, pass by. Stay on the path as it slowly descends. Box car park is at the bottom of the slope.

'Garden of Eden'

WALK 3   Bushy Willow

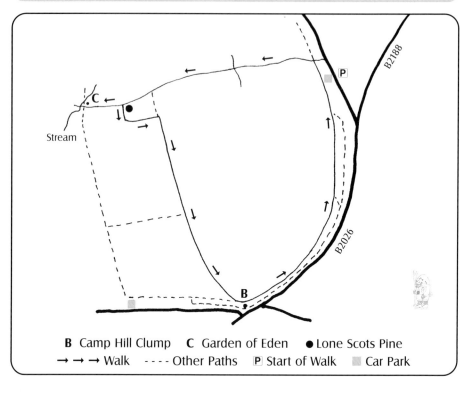

B Camp Hill Clump   **C** Garden of Eden   ● Lone Scots Pine
→ → → Walk   - - - - Other Paths   P Start of Walk   ▨ Car Park

Access/Parking:	Bushy Willow car park (page 7)
Map reference:	EX 135. 472303
Distance:	2½ - 3mls Combined 5 -6 mls.
Time:	2hrs Combined 4 -5 hrs
Terrain:	Wide paths. Steep hills. Muddy when wet. Can be strenuous.
Refreshments:	Nutley village 2mls on A22.

Points of Interest

B. Camp Hill Clump.
C. Garden of Eden.
Area named as it looks like an oasis. Pond fed by streams across Ashdown. Surrounded by Oak and Pine trees.

Combined Bushy Willow/Two Clumps & a Windmill.
A. Friends' Clump. (Walk 2)
B. Camp Hill Clump.
C. Garden of Eden.
D. Windmill. (Walk 2)
Oldest Post mill in Sussex. Finished work in 1908. Renovated 1968. In 1972 became a working mill again. Size 15ft high, 10ft wide, making it a small example. Opening details page 12.

Route directions
Walk to the back of the car park.

Take the path sloping down slightly. After 300-400m come into main path. Turn right.

Follow path for about ½ mile. Come to a gate and car park. Turn left. Follow path downhill. Path ahead in the distance is where you will be walking.

Carry on downhill. Passing woods on your left, fields of heather on right.

Carry on further downhill. Ground is eroded from weather and feet. Come to a stream. Pass over the bridge. Path now climbs steeply for about 300yds. Come out on to a flatter path.

Path goes through heather on the left, short walk back to the path started out on. Retrace steps back.

Carry on along main path. Now starting to slope down. Views from here are breathtaking. Paths in distance are where you will be walking.

Garden of Eden in view (C).

Before reaching Garden of Eden, a single Scots Pine acts as a beacon. Turn left here. Path takes you through fields of heather, up on to main junction, and Camp Hill Clump (B).

At the junction turn left. Carry along the main muddy path. The 5th turning off leads back to the car park.

Combined walk
Carry on down to Garden of Eden (C) and take the main path up to Friends' Clump (A), then Camp Hill Clump (B).

Or, carry on down to Garden of Eden (C). Bear right. Head for the Windmill (D). Then up to Friends' Clump (A), and back to Camp Hill Clump (B).

Well worth the scenery.

Directions as Two Clumps and a Windmill.

View across valley

WALK 4 Radio Station Walk

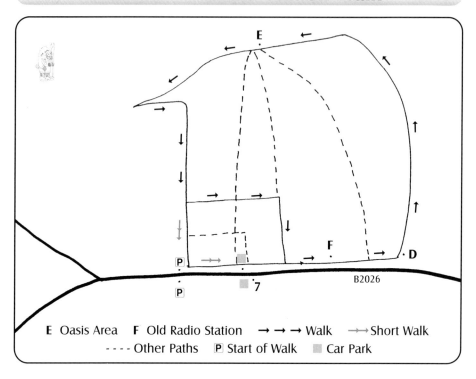

E Oasis Area   F Old Radio Station   → → → Walk   ⇝ Short Walk
- - - - Other Paths   P Start of Walk   ▓ Car Park

Access/Parking:	Pylons car park (page 7)
Map reference:	EX 135. 474298
Distance:	5-6mls
	(Short walk 4mls)
Time:	2½- 3₂hrs
	(Short walk 2hrs)
Terrain:	Wide paths. Steep hills. Muddy when wet.
Refreshments:	Nutley village about 1 ml from car park.

Points of interest

D. Crow's Nest Clump.
One of the original clumps planted in 1825. A major feature on the skyline. The damper ground here allows Cross-Leaved Heather, several mosses, and Bog Asphodel to be seen in the summer months in full bloom.

E. Oasis area.

F. Old Radio Station.
The area started out as an army camp in 1793.
It was taken over by the Diplomatic Corps Radio Station, code-named Aspidistra during

the 2nd World War, and used to make broadcasts as well as to transmit propaganda to Germany. Turned into a nuclear bunker in the 1950's. It is now a police training area.

Route directions

From Pylons car park, walk to the back of the second parking area.

Follow path leading off.

At the junction turn left. Follow the path down. Looking over the valley you will see spectacular views.

Path now starts to slowly climb. Ahead you can see Crow's Nest Clump (D).

As you make your way towards the clump you pass a fenced off area on the right. This is the Old Radio Station (F).

Still on the wide grass path, it comes to a junction.

Take left fork.

Pick up walk from Poundgate car park.

Walk around clump (D) skirted with heather bushes, and look onto a tiny wilderness area.

Path now goes downhill.

On each side (in summer) a carpet of reds and yellows intermingled with heather and grass, accompany your steps.

Before reaching the valley floor, an Oasis (E) can be seen.

Evergreens, Scots Pine and Silver Birch surround a pool to allow the wildlife to drink in safety.

Passing by/through the Oasis, take the left fork.

Looking up the path looks daunting from the bottom. A slow climb up allows you to relish the sights and views as more of the valley floor is seen as you climb.

Once at the top, there are two paths.

Short walk

Carry straight on.

The outer path takes you round to the car park, on a flat path.

Long walk

Turn left, heading in through heather and bracken.

Carry on downhill.

Turn right at the junction.

Now the path climbs back up to the Old Radio Station (F).

At this point turn right, back up the hill, to the car park.

WALK 5   Eastern Clumps

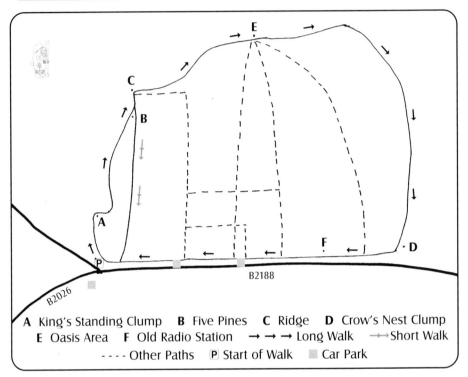

A King's Standing Clump **B** Five Pines **C** Ridge **D** Crow's Nest Clump
E Oasis Area **F** Old Radio Station → → → Long Walk ⟶ Short Walk
- - - - Other Paths Ⓟ Start of Walk ▨ Car Park

Access/Parking:	King's Standing car park (page 7)
Map reference:	EX 135. 473302
Distance:	Short walk ³/₄ml. Long walk, extension of Radio Station walk in opposite direction. Approx 6mls.
Time:	Short walk 30mins. Long walk 3hrs.
Terrain:	Short walk, flat wide paths. Can be muddy. Suitable for all. Long walk, steep hills. Wide paths. Can be strenuous.
Refreshments:	On B2188 at bottom of hill. Half Moon Inn.

Points of interest
As Radio Station walk.

A. King's Standing Clump.
This area is known for the fact that Henry VIII used it as a raised shooting box (a high seat) when shooting game as it passed.

B. Five Pines.
Area where 5 ancient but elegant pines adorn the skyline.

C. Ridge.

D. Crow's Nest Clump.

E. Oasis area.

F. Old Radio Station.

Route directions

This walk is an extension of the Radio Station walk.

Starting from the car park, walk in an easterly direction towards King's Standing Clump (A).

Scots Pine trees standing tall, mature. They could tell their own stories.

Look out for the skylark overhead as you walk around the back of the clump.

View from Five Pines Ridge down

Now turn left. Follow the wide grass flat path. You go through a gorse area. Then the path opens up on to a heather ridge. Ahead you can see five Scots Pine trees (B).

Go on for about another 100m to the peak of the ridge (C).

Now a long walk, Radio Station or short walk.

Long walk carry on down the hill to the oasis (E) and back up, walking in the opposite direction to Radio Station walk.

Short walk turn sharp right at the peak, staying on the flat. A thin parallel path brings you back to King's Standing Clump and the car park.

Section of Five Pines Ridge

WALK 6   Pooh Walk

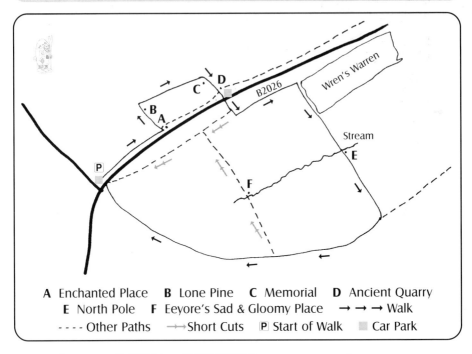

A Enchanted Place   **B** Lone Pine   **C** Memorial   **D** Ancient Quarry
E North Pole   **F** Eeyore's Sad & Gloomy Place   → → → Walk
- - - - Other Paths   ⊶ Short Cuts   **P** Start of Walk   ▨ Car Park

Access/Parking: Gill's Lap car park (page 7)

Map reference: EX 135. 467315

Distance: 4-5mls
(Short walk 1½mls)

Time: 2-3hrs
(Short walk ½-¾ - 1hr)

Terrain: A lot of climbing can make long walk strenuous. Muddy paths when wet. Short walk on easy wide paths. Only one hill.

Refreshments: B2188 2mls.
Half Moon Inn.

Points of interest

A. Gill's Lap Clump
Christopher Robin called this place 'The Enchanted Place'. So named because nobody was ever able to count the exact number of trees there.

B. Lone Pine.
Be careful as you approach 'The Lone Pine'.
Do not fall into the 'Heffalump Trap' beneath the tree.

C. Memorial.
This area is a memorial to A.A. Milne, the author, and E.H. Shepard, the illustrator, of Winnie the Pooh books.

D. Ancient Quarry.
The ancient quarry is now filled with water. Ancient trees

surround an oasis and wildlife extravaganza, an area not to be missed.

E. North Pole.

Try not to fall in like Roo. Your helpers may not have a stick to get you out.

F. Eeyore's Gloomy place.

Route directions

Take the wide path at the back of the car park. Follow the path along until you come to a clump of trees. Gill's Lap Clump (Enchanted Place) (A) .

Leaving the clump, turn sharp left, downhill.

You now come down to the Lone Pine (B).

Standing on the 'Lookout Ridge', the views across the North Downs are spectacular.

From the Lone Pine (B) follow the steep path, downhill, to the main path. Turn right.

Follow the main grassy heather path as it climbs, and slowly bends.

Look over and above to your right. You will see a wooden fenced area.

This is the memorial area.

Walk through this memorial area (C).

As you leave the memorial, turn left, joining the main path. Cross over and you come to the Ancient Quarry (D). The small pool to the side is Roo's sandy pit, now filled with water.

Follow the path on up, and then down into Quarry car park.

Cross over the road. Follow the small path opposite, to the main path. Turn left. Stay on the wide grass/mud path as it bears right passing through Wren's Warren heading downhill towards a stream. This is the site of the North Pole (E).

Once over the stream, steep path leads uphill through a Pine Alley.
Rest and absorb the views.
At the top turn right. Follow the path as it curves round and climbs.
Looking into the valley bottom is a boggy area called Eeyore's Sad and Gloomy Place (F).
Follow the grass/heather path as it curves round and heads back towards the car park.

Short cut walking through Eeyore's Sad and Gloomy Place
Looking down into Eeyore's Gloomy place, turn left, at the top of the hill, on to a wide grass path.
Follow the path leading downhill.
When you reach the point where the path turns left, carry on down into the valley.
Bear left, on a smaller path.
Cross the stream on grass stepping stones. Carry on back uphill on the grass path. This can be muddy and slippery. This path brings you up to a wider path.
Turn left. You are going uphill beside the road.
Path brings you back to the car park.
The thrill of walking in Eeyore's Sad and Gloomy place (F) is inspiring.

Short walk
Follow details from the car park, to the quarry.
You visit The Enchanted Place (A), The Lone Pine (B), then round to the memorial stone (C).
On past the ancient quarry (D) then through Quarry car park, to the road.
Turn right.
Follow the wide grass path, beside the road, then back uphill.
This path leads back to Gill's Lap car park.

Roo's sandy pit, now pond area

Wren's Warren

WALK 7   Ridge Walk

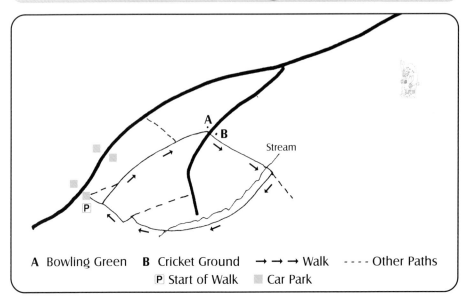

A Bowling Green   **B** Cricket Ground   → → → Walk   - - - - Other Paths
                                    P Start of Walk   ▪ Car Park

Access/Parking:	Ridge car park (page 9)
Map reference:	EX 135. 442325
Distance:	4mls
Time:	2hrs
Terrain:	Steep slopes. Woodland area, difficult walking as tree roots form path. Slippery when wet. Not suitable as a stroll.
Refreshments:	Wych Cross Tea Rooms ½ml.

Points of interest

A. Bowling green.

B. Cricket ground.

In this area you will see examples of Sphagnum Mosses, and look out for that elusive deer track, even deer.

Panoramic views across the Downs are well worth the walk.

Route directions

Walk to the back of the car park. Follow path straight on until you come to the main wide path.

Turn left.

Follow grass/mud path as it slopes down and veers to the left, then right.

Reaching the flat at the bottom, see woodland of Birch and Oak that guide you on until you reach a tarmac road.

Now Coleman's Hatch bowling green is on your left, and the cricket pitch is on your right.

Cross over and follow the path to the right of the pitch.

Woodland each side of the sandy soil path guides you downhill, then follow on to a grass path as it curves around.

The path now comes out on to a wider mud path.

Here turn right, going downhill.

At the bottom, you come to a stream.

Cross over on the bridge.

After about 20m, climbing up, a small path veers off to the right into deep woods.

Follow the path along the top of the bank, now becoming thinner, through dense woodland of Oak, Birch, Evergreen and Holly. Watch those roots.

As the path winds, you are slowly climbing, with the stream on your right.

Where the path divides off veer to the right hand side, with the stream still as your guide.

Once out of the woods, you come on to a wider stone path.

Turn right.

You now pass through an area of Scots Pine trees.

Following the path round, now grass, you come back up on to the main path.

Straight over the 'crossroads' paths, and back into the car park.

WALK 8   Hollies Down

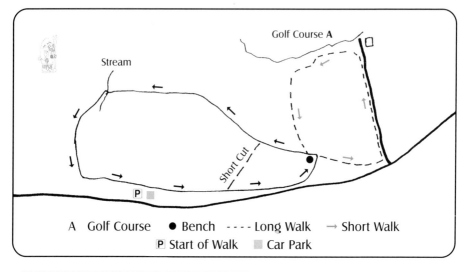

A Golf Course   ● Bench   - - - - Long Walk   → Short Walk
P Start of Walk   ▨ Car Park

Points of interest

A. Golf course.

On the golf course, in long grass, mushrooms of different varieties and colours are seen in autumn.

An enjoyable walk through different landscapes

Access/Parking:	Linton's car park (page 9)
Map reference:	EX 135. 442326
Distance:	5mls (Short walk 2½mls)
Time:	2½hrs (Short walk 1¼hrs)
Terrain:	Wide paths. Muddy when wet. Long walk, down steep slope, up through heavy gorse. Steep slope back up to car park on both walks.
Refreshments:	Wych Cross Tea Rooms ¾ml.

Route directions

From the back of the car park, go straight on to the main path.
Turn right. Once on the flat, stay on the path as it winds. Turn left at the junction.
A slight dip leads you towards a clump of trees. Come to the bench on your left.
Bench landmark.

Long walk

Turn right at the bench. Follow path as it twists, and slowly climbs. Come to a crossroads of cobbled paths.

Turn left. Go down the steep cobbled path through the woods of Oak, Silver Birch and Holly, with bracken underfoot. It leads on to a mud path passing a house and on to part of the golf course. Turn left.

Keep to the side of the golf course. Follow the contour of the land, slowly climbing.

You now come to the flag area on the golf course. Walk around the back of the flag position.

Look for the path going through the trees.

Take this path. Look out for path on left, starting with man-made steps leading up. Take this path.

Walking through ferns and bracken, often as tall as yourself, there is a well-worn path underfoot.

A steep climb up brings you out opposite the bench. Rest and absorb the views across the valley.

Now follow the directions of the short walk, to complete the long walk.

Bench landmark.

Short walk

From bench keep left.

Wide path meanders slowly down, through bracken and heather, with landscape views.

Stay on the path as it descends quickly, heading into woods.

At the bottom you come to a stream.

Cross over on a wooden-slatted bridge.

Stay on a wide mud path, as it slowly climbs, crossing another stream.

Then the path drops.

You are now walking beside the stream.

Coming out of the woods, the path bears left. Coming out into the open, ahead is a wide path heading up, which is a steep climb.

Take a slow wander up, stopping to digest the views, this brings you up on to the flat. Turn left.

Carry on along the wide path back to the junction of the car park.

WALK 9   Old Airstrip

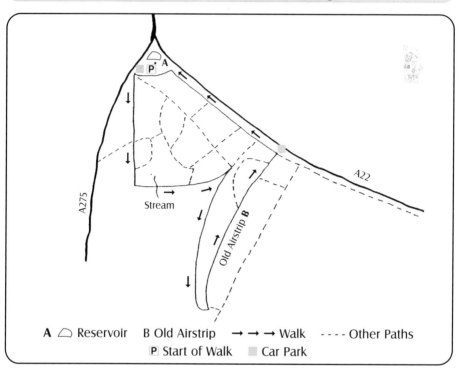

A ⌂ Reservoir   B Old Airstrip   → → → Walk   - - - - Other Paths
P Start of Walk   ▨ Car Park

Access/Parking:	Reservoir car park (page 8)
Map reference:	EX 135. 420317
Distance:	3-3½mls
Time:	1½- 2hrs
Terrain:	Flat walking. Wide paths. Only one slight hill. Suitable for all ages. Boggy when wet.
Refreshments:	Wych Cross Tea Rooms ½ml.

Points of interest

A. Reservoir.

B. Old Airstrip.

The airstrip was built by the Canadians in World War II as an exercise.

As a wet heath area it is known for Purple Moor Grass, Bog Cotton, Bog Asphodel, Cross-leaved Heather.

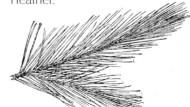

Route directions

From the car park, go past the pole barrier.

Follow the main wide sandy/mud path.

Do not turn off.

Carry on for another 20mins walking in between bracken and heather. Look out for a fenced field.

At this junction turn left, with the field on your right.

Walk downhill and cross over the bridge.

Now slowly climb up on to open heathland.

Carry on past junctions on your left, until you come to an area of many junctions.

Take the first right.

As you walk along, on your left is an important area of wet heath.

The path comes out to a 'T' junction. Turn left, this is the old airstrip.

As you walk along the strip on a sandy pathway, look out for Ling heather, Gorse and young Scots Pine, dotted in areas where other plants cannot survive due to the drier soil.

At the end of the path, you come into a car park. Turn left.

Follow the wide mud path, alongside the main road.

Walking through woodland of Oak, Beech, Hawthorn, Willow and Holly, a vast array of colours in summer and autumn, the path veers to the left.

Follow this path, and you are now walking at the back of the reservoir.

Follow the path round, and back into the car park.

Old Airfield

WALK 10 Old Lodge Nature Reserve

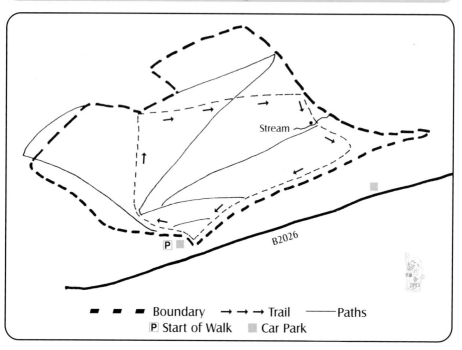

— — — Boundary → → → **Trail** ——**Paths**
P Start of Walk ▦ **Car Park**

Points of interest

Avenue of Scots Pine trees.
Autumn is a picturesque time for the varying pathways of trees.
Wild Deer.
Wild Exmoor ponies.
Boggy area allows the Black Darter and Golden Ringed Dragonflies to thrive in late summer.
Breathtaking views across the Downs.
Watch and listen for birds in spring and summer, flying overhead or in the undergrowth.

Access/Parking:	Lodge car park (page 7)
Map reference:	EX 135. 470306
Distance:	3¹⁄₂mls
Time:	2hrs
Terrain:	Steep up/down hills. Boggy area on up-climb. Wide paths. Muddy when wet. Stiles.
Refreshments:	B2188 2mls Half Moon Inn. B2026 Garden Centre 1¹⁄₂mls.

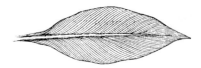

Route directions

At the back of the car park, go down the path, up some steps and through a gate into the Reserve.

Turn left.

Walking slowly downhill, on a wide grass path, it runs beside the boundary fence.

Follow this path down to the fence.

Climb over the stile.

Follow the path down.

Scots Pine, Oak and Ash trees accompany you, with bracken undergrowth.

Now on the flat, path veers off to the right.

You come to a wide grass path, with Scots Pine trees on each side of you. This is the Avenue.

Follow the path as it slowly climbs.

Walk right to the top and over the ridge.

You come to an area of green fields.

Turn right.

You are now in an area where deer are seen.

Keep a sharp look out, they are there.

As the path narrows, it descends steeply, passing ancient Chestnut trees bearing their roots from years of erosion of soil.

On reaching the fence, ignore the paths left/right. Go over the stile.

Path continues on down steeply. View across is the path going up.

Exmoor ponies

At the bottom, cross over the stream.

Now a well trodden muddy path climbs extremely steeply for about 50m.

Then still climbing up, you come into a Silver Birch and Scots Pine walk.

This is deer area. Keep a look out for a fleeting sight of a beautiful animal.

Half way up the path look out for a boggy area.

Dragonflies breed here in the summer and autumn, encouraging rare species to grow.
Carry on up.

Now a bench nestling in amongst Scots Pine comes into view. A welcome sight.

Stay on the wide path as it guides you on up the hill.

Follow the path round.

Coming out on to the flat, the area is more open.

Wild Exmoor ponies can be seen grazing, they help to keep the bracken down.

Follow the path, staying beside the boundary fence. You come back round to the car
park. A nature and wildlife extravaganza.

View across valley walked

Stream at bottom of Old Lodge path

WALK 11   Double Stream Dip

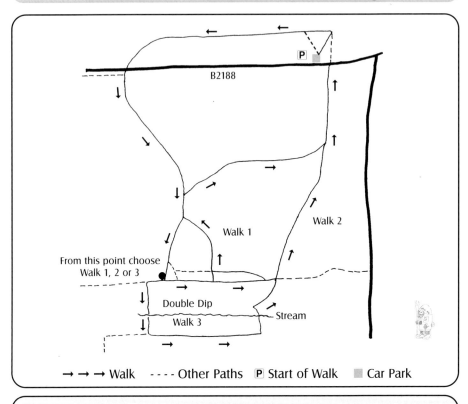

B2188

From this point choose
Walk 1, 2 or 3

Walk 1

Walk 2

Double Dip

Walk 3

Stream

→ → → Walk   - - - - Other Paths   P Start of Walk   ▮ Car Park

Access/Parking: Church Hill car park (page 7)

Map reference: EX 135. 495327

Distance: Walk One 3mls.
Walk Two 3½mls.
Walk Three 5mls.

Time: Walk One 2hrs.
Walk Two 2½hrs.
Walk Three 3½hrs.

Terrain: Walks 1, 2, are suitable for all. Wide paths. Some hills. Boggy when wet. Walk 3 is the double stream dip. Could get wet feet without wellies. Through dense woods, and steep climb.

Refreshments: Half Moon Inn ¼ml.

Points of interest

Views across the valley are breathtaking.

Follow instructions regarding the walk taking in Double Stream Dip.

Through the woods, go down to the stream. Be wary at wintertime. Stream can be high, and fast flowing.

Crossing over, then over another crossing, all the time trying not to get wet.

Route directions

Walk to the back of the car park. Path on right leads into woodland of Oak and Silver Birch.

Path comes out on to main grass path. Turn left.

Oak, Chestnut, and Holly trees escort you as the path slowly climbs, and thins. In wet weather, muddy conditions add to the relief of reaching a concrete path, and gate.

Turn right. Head down hill, staying on the path, until you reach the road. Cross over the road.

Take a left turn. Follow the path as it heads downhill.

You are now on a sand path, which can be slippery in wet weather. A wooded area of Chestnut, Oak and Cobnut trees, guides you down. Now the area opens up.

Follow the path around the side of bracken fields as you still descend.

As the path forks, take the right fork coming on to the concrete path, you now decide which route to take 1, 2, or 3 which is the double dip.

Walk 1

Turn left on the concrete path.

Walk along the path until you come to a grass path.

Take the second wide path on the left, and you come back to the open bracken area where you came down. Walk across field, to the top corner.

A small path leads you through trees on to a wide grass path. Turn left, going uphill.

Path comes out onto the road, opposite the car park.

Walk 2

Turn left on the concrete path, carry on to the third left turn.

Wide grass path leads uphill, carry on uphill till reaching the road, car park is opposite.

Walk 3

Double Dip Cross over the concrete path, bear right. Go down small mud path on the left leading into wooded area. Stay on the path, as it winds through dense woodland. Still going down, the path leads to a stream.

Find a place to cross. (Where the path leads to is crossable). If going downstream, come back to point of path on the opposite bank.

Head uphill on mud path, coming out of the woods to a wide grass path.

Turn left, follow the wide path as it bears left, and starts to go downhill back to the woods. Now on a muddy path, it's slippery when wet, it takes you back down to the stream, cross over again (2nd dip) and follow the path uphill climbing very steeply for about 20m, then turns. Now on a sand/mud path, follow it around the bend, and up to the grass path, where you pick up walks 1 and 2 to the car park.

WALK 12 Shepherds Stroll

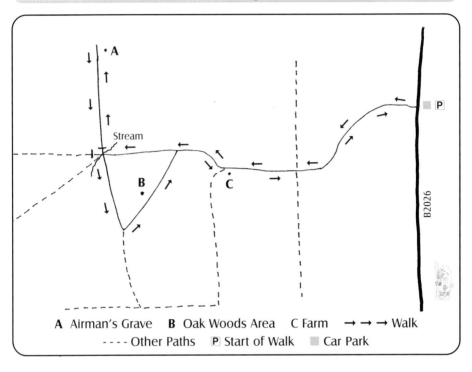

A Airman's Grave **B** Oak Woods Area C Farm → → → Walk
- - - - Other Paths P Start of Walk ▓ Car Park

Access/Parking:	Shepherds car park (page 6)
Map reference:	EX 135. 466272
Distance:	3mls.
Time:	1½hrs.
Terrain:	Some steep climbs. Muddy when wet. Wide paths.
Refreshments:	Duddleswell Tea Rooms ½ml.

Points of interest

A. Airman's Grave.

B. Oak Woods.

C. Farm.

Route directions

Come out of the car park, cross over the road and go through the gate directly opposite.

Follow the thin grass path hewn out between heather/bracken as it leads downhill.

At the bottom of the hill, you come to the main junction. Wide paths lead off.

Take the wide mud path opposite into woods of Oak, Chestnut and Evergreens.

Once through the mud in wet weather, solid earth in dry, you come to another junction.

Staying on a concrete path, pass a farm on your left, take the right fork.

You are now on a gullied wide sand/mud path, caused by erosion, heading down hill.

Over half way down, the path drops more quickly.

At this point, you can see the bottom, with its magical stream flowing, and the bridges. Make your way to the bottom.

In summer this is an ideal place to rest and soak the feet.

From the stream, turn directly right, over the first bridge.

Path leads sharply uphill, coming out of woods, on to open bracken/heather pastures.

Airman's Grave site is about 400m up. After visiting, come back downhill.

Cross over bridge, and take the second turn on your left from the bridge. (First path after path down). Path climbs steeply for 20 - 30m, then still climbs but slower.

On your left, up the bank, you are looking into an Oak wood (B). Bracken undergrowth helps hide the wildlife which can be heard, but not seen.

Staying on the path bear left at the junction. Turn right at the next junction.

You are now on the path, going back uphill, towards the farm (C). Carry straight on.

Coming out into an open bracken field, look opposite for the small grass path leading back uphill to the gate and car park.

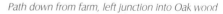

Path down from farm, left junction into Oak wood

WALK 13   Shepherds Walk

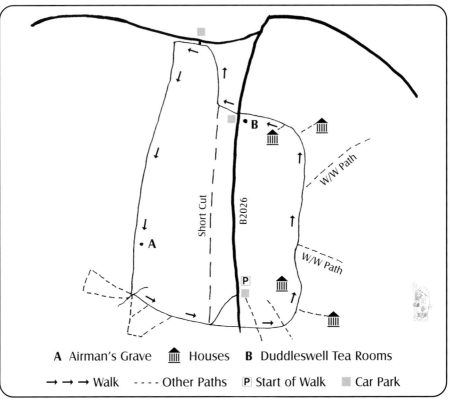

A Airman's Grave   🏛 Houses   **B** Duddleswell Tea Rooms

→ → → Walk   - - - - Other Paths   **P** Start of Walk   ▦ Car Park

Access/Parking:	Shepherds car park (page 6)
Map reference:	EX 135. 466272
Distance:	5mls. This walk can be extended to 7-8mls.
Time:	2½hrs. Extended walk 4hrs.
Terrain:	90% uphill. Not suitable for a stroll. Well worth the views. Lots of stamina. Paths muddy when wet.
Refreshments:	Duddleswell Tea Rooms ½ml.

Points of interest
A. Airman's Grave.

B. Duddleswell Tea Rooms.

Views across Downs are spectacular.

Route directions

From the car park, cross over the road. Go through the gate.

Follow the path downhill, through heather and bracken field, to a junction. Take the path first left, back uphill. Come out onto the road. Cross over. Follow the path as you wander through a corridor of Holly and Gorse bushes. Come to a junction.

Carry straight on.

Oak trees, with bracken undergrowth, now accompany your steps on the sand/mud path.

Now pass another junction, and start to descend.

As you turn the corner, a steep drop brings you to a stream.

Once over the bridge, the walk is a steady climb for the next 30+ mins.

As you climb, a junction shows the Weald Way Path has joined the main path.

Passing a house on your left, cross over the small gravel road. Oak and bracken still abound each side of the path like a corridor.

As the path continues to climb, its twisting action leads you into a new landscape.

Now the path opens up on to more heather and bracken.

A junction on the right is the Weald Way Path.

Carry straight on up.

Passing houses set back, cross another tiny concrete road.

Now the path flattens out.

Take a short breather.

Path leads out on to the road. Duddleswell tea rooms are 20m down on the left.

View across valley on main walk

39

Back to the walk. Cross over the road, go through the gate and follow the path uphill towards the Oak trees. Once through the woods the path brings you out into the open.

Short cut
Turn left, go downhill. The main grass path leads back to the main junction.
Now turn left back uphill, through the heather field, to the road.
Cross over to the car park.

Main walk
Once in the open turn right going uphill again. Follow the path as it twists.
Once at the top, bear left. Follow the path round, as it dips into a car park.

From the car park you can extend your walk another 2-3 miles. Carry on through the car park. Follow the wide grass path you can see, as it heads round and downhill, to the stream. Now follow main walk directions.

Back to the main walk
Turn left downhill beside the car park. The path leads down to the Airman's Grave (A).
Once at the bottom of the hill, bear left, and cross the stream.
Take the first left, uphill. It's almost the last hill. This hill is very steep.
Once at the top, pass the farm, and follow the mud path which leads back to the main junction. From this junction is your last climb.
Up through the heather field, to the road, and the car park.

Path down to Airman's grave

Path going uphill on Shepherds Walk

WALK 14   223M Exploration

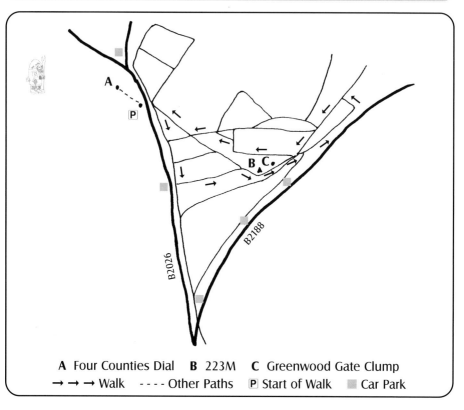

A Four Counties Dial   **B** 223M   **C** Greenwood Gate Clump
→ → → Walk   - - - - Other Paths   P Start of Walk   ▦ Car Park

Access/Parking:	Four Counties car park (page 7)
Map reference:	EX 135. 469312
Distance:	4mls.
Time:	2hrs.
Terrain:	Climbing steep hill. Wide paths. Slippery when wet.
Refreshments:	B2188 Half Moon Inn 2mls. Nutley village 4mls.

Points of interest

A. Four Counties Dial.
About 200m along from the car park a concrete pillar houses the Four Counties Dial. This was placed here to celebrate the Queen's Silver Jubilee in 1977.

B. 223m. Stunning views from this point.

C. Greenwood Gate Clump.
One of the eight original Clumps planted in 1825.

Route directions to Four Counties Dial. From the back of the car park turn right. Follow well-trodden path through heather and return the same way.

Route directions

Come out of the car park by the way in.

Cross over the road, walk along about 50m.

Coming to the wide sandy path, turn right and follow the path, as it follows the road.

Ignore the first turning left. Carry straight on.

Seeing a car park on the opposite side of the road, take the left turn here.

Climbing up, high gorse bushes are on the left, heather fields on the right form a distinctive alleyway.

Go straight over at the junction, still climbing.

You are now standing on the highest point in Ashdown Forest, 223m high (B).

Once on the flat, bear right.

Path goes around Greenwood Gate Clump (C).

Coming out on to a main wide sandy path, carry straight on.

You are in an avenue of Gorse on your left and Scots Pine trees to your right.

Carry straight on.

Path leads to a T-junction.

All along this path Oaks form a corridor.

Now the path joins up with Weald Way Path.

Turn left going uphill.

You are heading back up towards the Greenwood Gate Clump (C).

Turn right at the third junction.

Now turn left at the next junction.

Bear left at the following junction, as you once again climb up for a short while.

Once back on the top, you can see the paths leading down. The views are stunning.

Follow the path downhill, as it leads back to the starting point, opposite the Four Counties car park.

Paths shown on map can shorten this walk.

Four Counties Dial

WALK 15   Clumps/Warren/North Pole

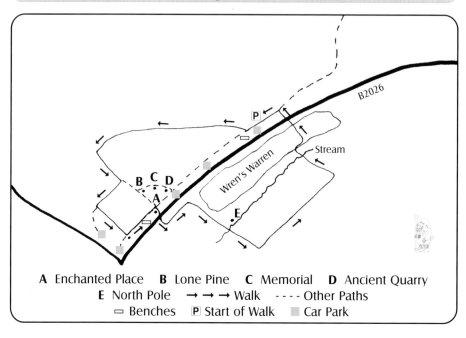

A Enchanted Place   **B** Lone Pine   **C** Memorial   **D** Ancient Quarry
E North Pole   → → → Walk   - - - - Other Paths
▭ Benches   Ⓟ Start of Walk   ▨ Car Park

Access/Parking:	Wren's Warren car park (page 7)
Map reference:	EX 135. 471326
Distance:	5mls.
Time:	2½hrs.
Terrain:	Wide paths. Muddy when wet. Steep hills. A lot of climbing. Not suitable for a stroll.
Refreshments:	Hartfield village 2mls. Coleman's Hatch 2mls.

Points of interest

A. Gill's Lap Clump (Enchanted Place).

B. Lone Pine.

C. Memorial.

D. Ancient Quarry.

E. North Pole.

Route directions

Take the path behind the log, near the entrance.
After 20m on a mud path, you come out on to a junction beside a bench.
Looking up the hill, is the start of your walk.

Bear right at the bench. Stay on the wide mud path as it climbs.

Before reaching the top, bear left, at the junction.

Once at the top, turn left at T-junction.

Still climbing, your path is a gorse and bracken corridor. To your right is open valley, to your left deep woods. The contrast is spectacular in its own way.

On reaching the flat T-junction at the top, turn right.

Path starts flat, then slowly climbs.

On your left look out for a copse of Wild Oak trees.

Path comes to a junction.

Turn left.

Another steep uphill climb on a muddy path. Stop and absorb the views all around, or wait until you reach the top.

A welcome bench awaits the weary walker at the top.

Turn left at the bench. (as facing) Path is on the flat. You come to another bench.

From here the path directs you to Gill's Lap Clump (Enchanted Place) (A).

Walk around/through clump, and take path opposite going downhill.

'Pooh' extras can be added to walk here.

A short distance down the path, cross the road.

The view at this point is Wren's Warren Valley (E).

An impressive sight. Firs, Evergreen trees, with bracken and heather, give an openness to the area.

'North Pole' stream

45

20m down hill, turn left at the junction on to a wide grass/mud path.

Carry along on the flat, until path bears right, going downhill.

Follow the path down. Your return path uphill looms before you.

Follow the path all the way down to the stream at the bottom. It is a pleasant resting place. Cross the stream by the bridge.

Path now climbs. A Fir tree and bracken corridor guide you up the steep incline.

Reaching the top, turn left.

Path is again on the flat.

Open fields of heather and grasses have crept onto the path to give the impression of a carpet of exquisite colour.

Path starts to slowly descend.

Ignore right turn.

Carry on down.

Looking across the valley, the buildings seen were used to house refugees in the Second World War, they are now kennels and private homes.

Turn left at the junction, going down on a more muddy steep path to the stream.

Again another pleasant stopping place.

Cross the stream using stepping stones in the water.

Bear left with the path, as you again climb up steeply.

Path bears right.

Now there is only one mud path which twists as it progresses through a section of Five Hundred Acre Wood. It is here that you see the damage done by the 1987 storm, along with ancient and new growth of Oak trees, which nestle in between swaths of bracken. This path brings you out on to the road.

Path down through Wren's Warren

Gill's Lap Clump, or Enchanted Place

Cross over.

Follow mud path as it bears left climbing up.

You pass an area enclosed by a fence.

Point to pick up Extended Pooh walk.

Carry on up the hill.

A short cut back to the car park is cut through the bracken undergrowth on your left.

If not carry on back to the bench where you started and return by the path at the back of the bench.

Well worth the effort, if possible. The scenery surpasses itself.

WALK 16 Extended Pooh Walk

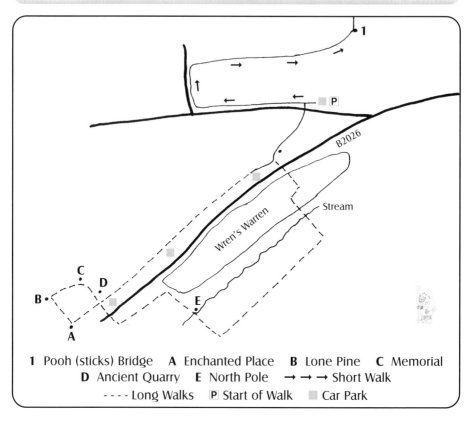

1 Pooh (sticks) Bridge **A** Enchanted Place **B** Lone Pine **C** Memorial
D Ancient Quarry **E** North Pole → → → Short Walk
- - - - Long Walks P Start of Walk ▨ Car Park

Access/Parking:	Pooh car park (page 7)
Map reference:	EX 135. 471333
Distance:	1½mls (Long walk 3-7mls).
Time:	¾hrs (Long walk 2-5hrs).
Terrain:	Short walk: paths flat. Steps, suitable for all, muddy when wet. Long walk: as short walk, with steep climbing, wide paths. As other Pooh walks.
Refreshments:	Hartfield village 1½mls.

Points of interest
1. Pooh (sticks) Bridge

Restored in 1979 and 1999, where you can throw Pooh sticks into the water, and watch them float downstream.

As previous Pooh walks.

A. Enchanted Place.

B. Lone Pine.

C. Memorial.

D. Ancient Quarry.

E. North Pole

Route directions
Short walk from Pooh car park

From the car park, follow the mud path through the woods.
As the path comes to a road, bear right down the road.
Pass Andbells house.
Carry on down the road for about 50m.
Turn right into a bridlepath.
Pass fields of a farm. Carry on down a concrete path as it twists, and thins out.
Path now goes down as steps. Once at the bottom, carry on through the woods on a concrete/mud path.
Path leads to Pooh (sticks) Bridge.
Retrace your steps back to Pooh car park.

Pooh (sticks) Bridge

49

Long walk

Pooh (sticks) Bridge can also be reached from Wren's Warren car park.

Take the wide path at the back of the car park.

Turn left downhill onto a wide mud path, bear left, going through a fenced area.

Carry on down the path and take the left fork towards houses, now on a grass path.

Come out on to a concrete road. Stay on the road until it comes out onto a main road.

Turn left, then first right.

The road brings you to Andbells.

Follow Pooh (sticks) Bridge route.

Retrace steps back to Wren's Warren car park.

Extended long walk

This walk includes all the areas of Pooh.

Start from Pooh car park.

Head for Pooh (sticks) Bridge and return on the long route to Wren's Warren car park.

Stay on the wide path.

Now follow the directions of Clumps/Warren/North Pole - Walk 15.

Children throwing 'Pooh' sticks in the water

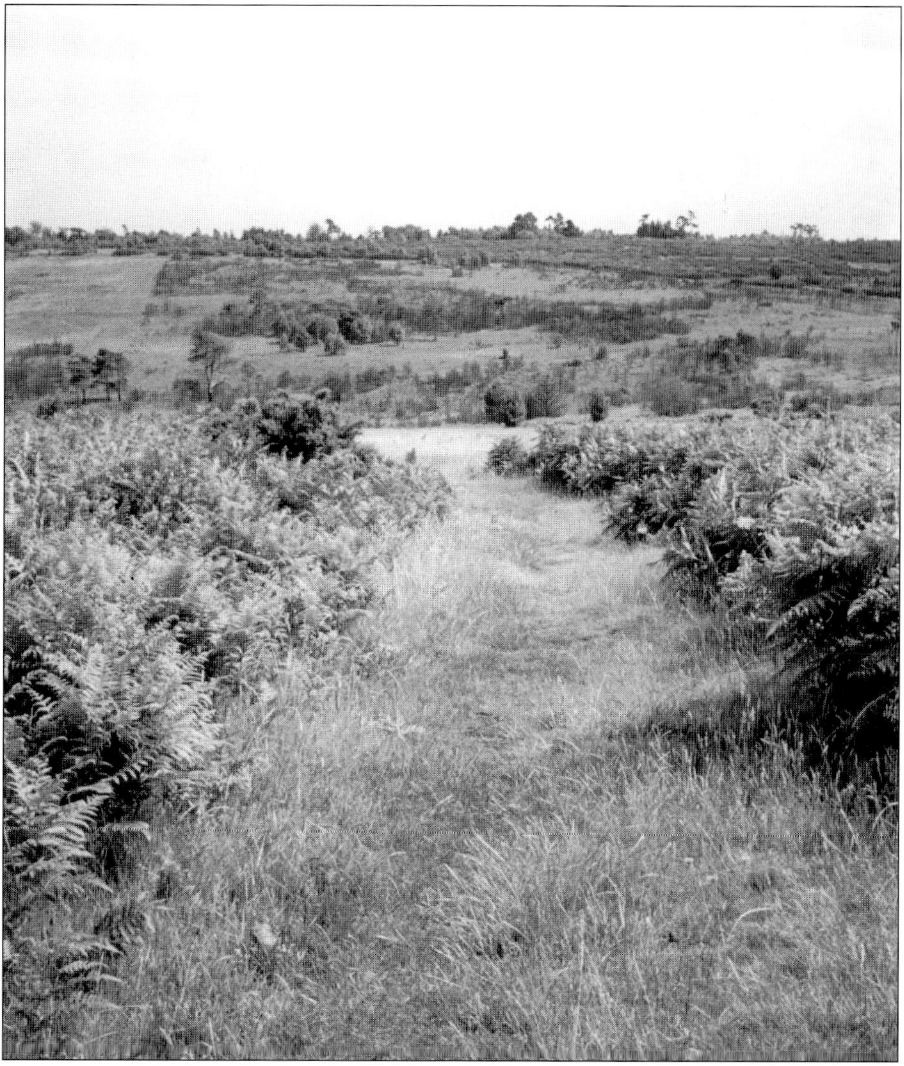

Wren's Warren area

WALK 17   Plains/Woods Adventure

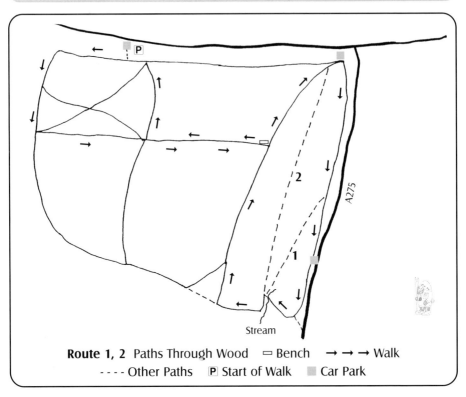

Route 1, 2 Paths Through Wood   ▭ Bench   → → → Walk
- - - - Other Paths   Ⓟ Start of Walk   ▨ Car Park

Access/Parking:	Hindleap car park (page 8)
Map reference:	EX 135. 405323
Distance:	½ml (Short walk)
	4 mls (Long walk)
Time:	30-45mins (Short walk)
	2hrs (Long walk)
Terrain:	Short walk, on open plains. Wide paths. Muddy when wet. Flattish. Long walk, steep hill, wide paths. Muddy in wet. Woods.
Refreshments:	Wych Cross Tea Rooms 1 ml.

Points of interest

A. Woods.

Open plains, showing off bracken, grasses and shrubs, giving an array of colours in summer, and varying browns in winter.

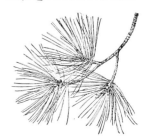

Route directions

From the car park veer to the right as you walk over the grass picnic area.

Reaching the main wide grass path, turn right.

Follow the path as it winds round to the left.

You are now walking on the open plain.

Carry on along the path until you come to a bench on your left.

Turn left, uphill.

The open plain is on your left, woods of Oak, Silver Birch and Scots Pine on your right. You can see well-worn paths in the woods. It is well worth the diversion to explore the immediate area for wildlife.

Back on the path.

As you proceed uphill, the mud path veers round to the right.

Left is Twyford car park.

Stay on the grass path as you walk into the woods, with a road on the left.

On your right, you are looking into the wooded valley, as the path has slowly climbed without really noticing.

Staying on the main path, you pass a car park, and a tiny path on your left.

A short distance on look out for a large Oak tree on the left.

Beside the tree a well worn path goes steeply down.

On reaching a tiny flat area, there are 3 paths leading off.

Take the 2nd off to the right, go through the woods you just walked past. Paths are marked on the map.

The third you can see through the trees.

It looks more daunting than it is.

Go on down, crossing a stream over a small wooden bridge. A sandy path veers round and up, it is not as steep as it first looks.

As you slowly climb up the path it bears right, leading out on to the open plain.

You are now back at the bench.

Turn left. Cross over the open plain.

Stay on the path until the junction.

Turn right. Climbing up you come out on to the main path.

Car park is across the open picnic area.

Ancient Oak tree, showing path to be walked

WALK 18 Shades Exploration

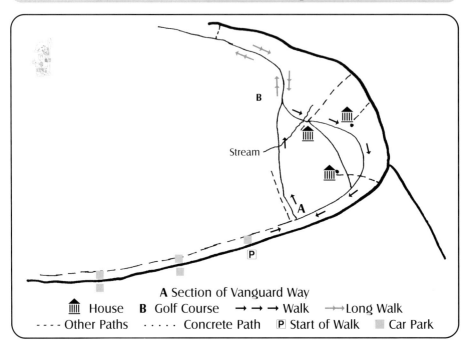

B

Stream

A

A Section of Vanguard Way

🏛 House **B** Golf Course → → → Walk →→Long Walk
- - - - Other Paths · · · · · Concrete Path Ⓟ Start of Walk ▦ Car Park

Access/Parking:	Shades car park (page 9)
Map reference:	EX 135. 445329
Distance:	3 mls (Short walk)
	5 mls (Long walk)
Time:	1½hrs (Short walk)
	2½hrs (Long walk)
Terrain:	Wide paths. Muddy when wet. Steep up and down.
Refreshments:	Nutley village 2 mls.

Points of interest

A. Section Of Vanguard Way.

B. Golf Course.

Woods and varying wildlife seen in the area.
Spectacular views.

Route directions

From the back of the car park, take the path bearing right through the trees.

You come out on to the main wide path.

Turn left, going downhill on a wide grass path. Come on to the flat.

Go straight over a concrete path.

A short way on, come to a junction and turn left.

Now on a section of the Vanguard Way (A).

Woods both sides of the wide grass path help guide you as the path twists going downwards.

Once at the bottom, a wooden bridge goes over a stream.

Cross and veer to the right, follow the path as it winds, you are now walking beside the golf course.

As the path bears to the right, more dense woods are on both sides.

Long walk

At the junction carry on along the path going through the woods.

Passing a house, the path descends, then comes out on to the flat. Now the golf course is in sight. Again carry on along to the road.

Now retrace your steps back uphill to the junction, and continue on the short walk.

Short walk

At the junction turn left, downhill. Cross over the road onto a mud path straight ahead.

Going downhill you cross the stream, coming to a junction.

The outside path goes uphill, the inside path starts off on the flat, passing in front of a house, and joins up with the outside path on the hill.

On the outside path climb a short way, and cross the stream once again. Coming out of the woods a house is in view.

Do not pass the house but turn right in front of the house down a small mud path.

Coming to a hedge, path veers to the right uphill. Carry on uphill, entering the woods again.

Once on the flat the path veers right. Stay on this path as it goes through the woods then crosses over a concrete path, and continue through dense woods of Oak and Chestnut, crossing a second concrete path

Follow the wide path as it starts to climb.

You are now retracing your route back to the car park.

WALK 19   A Quiet Wooded Walk

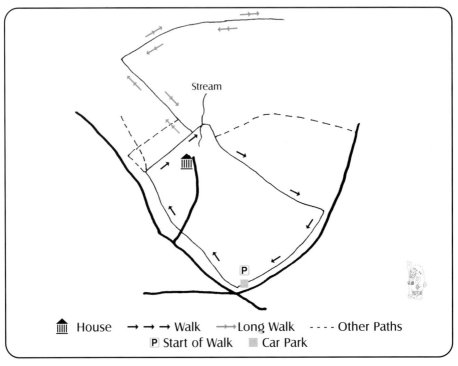

Stream

House → → → **Walk** →→**Long Walk** - - - - **Other Paths**
P Start of Walk   ▨ Car Park

Access/Parking:	Goat car park (page 9)
Map reference:	EX 135. 402326
Distance:	1¼ mls (Short walk)
	2¼ mls (Long walk)
Time:	45mins (Short walk)
	1½hrs (Long walk)
Terrain:	Muddy paths when wet. Wide grass, some stone paths. Long walk into woods. Short/Long walk, return steep uphill.
Refreshments:	Wych Cross Tea Rooms 2 mls.

Points of interest

Stream area allows Rushes and Sedge to grow.

Look out for Sphagnum Moss on path up from stream. Look for the Alder tree, beside the stream.

Autumn brings out varying fungi in this area.

Views across the Downs are worth the walk.

Route directions

From the back of the car park, follow the path to your left.
The narrow path leads through woods of Willow, Ash, Birch, Sycamore and Elder.
Crossing a road, carry on through the woods, until you come out on to open heathland.
Turn right, downhill.
Now on to a wide grass eroded path.
As you descend see the woods change.
Look out for mature heather, bracken, Birch and Pine trees.
Stay on this path as you pass the house, then bear left.
Come to a junction.

Long walk

At junction carry straight on, as the path thins out.
Walking in more dense woodland the path twists as it goes on down, then turns right.
Ignore public footpath signs. Bear right, carry on along the side of a bank.
Retrace your steps climbing hill, enjoying a second chance to see the nature and wildlife.
Back at the junction. Carry on with short walk.

Short walk

At junction turn right, going downhill.
Wide concrete path looks like it's going around a corner, follow the path around.
Coming to a stream, cross and turn left.
Stay on wide mud path as it climbs steeply, look out for fungi and other reeds in season.
Stay on the main path to the top.
Once at the top, path opens up on to heathland.
Just before the road, turn right.
Stay on the thin mud path as it guides you through the woods, with bracken and heathland flowers, for company.
This path takes you back to the car park.

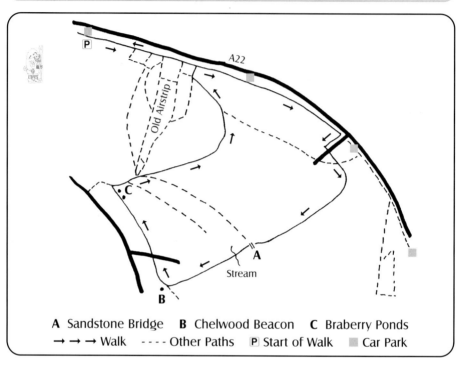

A Sandstone Bridge   **B** Chelwood Beacon   **C** Braberry Ponds
→ → → Walk   - - - - Other Paths   P Start of Walk   ▓ Car Park

Access/Parking:	Long car park (page 8)
Map reference:	EX 135. 428309
Distance:	5 mls.
Time:	2½ hrs.
Terrain:	Concrete paths. Wide grass paths. Clay paths. Can be muddy when wet. Steep climb up twice. Steep down. Not suitable for a stroll.
Refreshments:	Wych Cross Tea Rooms 1 ml. Ashdown Llama Farm (almost opposite).

Points of interest

A. Sandstone Bridge.

Just before this go through the gate on your left, and the path takes you on to the bridge.
Return the same way back to the path.

B. Chelwood Beacon.

C. Braberry Ponds.

Braberry ponds are a series of ornamental ponds running from the Isle of Thorns to Chelwood Vachery.

Route directions

From the car park, turn left on to the main path.

Follow the clay, mud path as it descends and climbs, passing Trees car park.

Path follows beside the A22.

Look out for the rabbits, and the elusive moles, both of which have left their own marks along the path.

On reaching a tarmac road, turn right.

30m in, turn left onto a smaller concrete path. Follow the path as it winds in between Oak and Scots Pine trees, bracken and heather.

Pass between outbuildings of Chelwood Vachery.

Path now starts to descend, with fencing on either side.

Nearing the bottom, woodland of Beech, Yew, and Holly is seen on either side.

Once at the bottom, you come to a sandstone bridge (A).

Back on the path, go under the bridge, and you come to a stream.

Stepping stones allow you to cross and carry on up the hill, opposite.

Look out for mature and young Pine trees. The path is leading up on to Chelwood Beacon (B).

Once at the top, turn right.

Carry on along the wide grass/mud path, crossing over a concrete path. Scots Pine adorn each side of the path.

As the path bears left, it dips steeply. Follow it down and cross a tiny bridge.

Braberry Ponds are now in front of you.

Turn left and walk around the first pond.

Second pond now comes into view.

Follow the path in between the ponds. Stay on the path bearing left around the second pond.

You are now slowly climbing, as the path winds between woods and bracken away from the ponds.

Coming out to a junction, turn right.

Wide clay, mud path climbs slowly.

Follow the path past boundary bank under some Pine trees.

Once on the top, turn left below the Pine clump.

Now take a right fork after 100m.

Follow this path as it descends then climbs, twisting as it goes.

This path guides you through Scots Pine trees as you climb up on to the main top path.

Once here turn left.

Back uphill to the car park.

Braberry Ponds

Path between ponds

WALK 21 Lintons Adventure

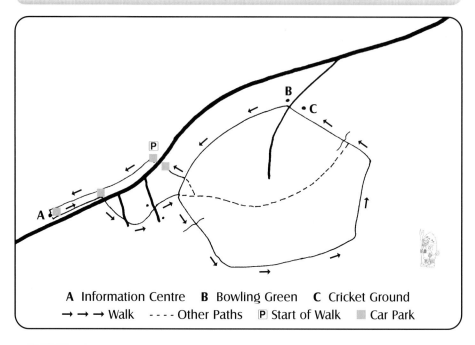

A Information Centre **B** Bowling Green **C** Cricket Ground
→ → → Walk - - - - Other Paths Ⓟ Start of Walk ▨ Car Park

Access/Parking:	Linton's car park (page 9)
Map reference:	EX 135. 442326
Distance:	4½ mls.
Time:	2½ hrs.
Terrain:	Wide grass paths. Clay paths. Slippery when wet. Some flat walking. Some climbing. Suitable for families. Not pushchairs.
Refreshments:	Wych Cross Tea Rooms ½ ml.

Points of interest

A. Information Centre

B. Bowling green.

C. Cricket ground.

This walk takes in parts of Walk 7, Ridge Walk.

Route directions

From the back of the car park, walk across the grass to a wide path. Turn left, uphill. Once at the top of the hill, stay on the main path. It changes from grass, with bracken and heather, to peat and pine needles.

This path brings you to the Information Centre (A).

Bear right in the car park, heading back on another peat/pine needle path.

You come into Broadstone car park.

Now cross over the road, picking up a wide grass path.

Scots Pine trees on both sides of the path guide you as the path comes out into the open.

Cross over the concrete path, carry straight on, passing a house on the left, then a house on the right.

Bear left on the grass path downhill and stay on the path with woods now on the right and an open expanse of heather and bracken on the left.

At the junction turn right, downhill, heading into the woods.

Oak and Holly trees, with thick bracken undergrowth, accompany you as the path zigzags downhill.

Near the bottom a steep incline brings you to a stream.

Cross over and climb up the steep bank before the path levels out more.

Looking into the valley on your left, the stream is seen with a path running beside it. (This path is mentioned in Walk 7).

Look out for deer tracks, even deer as you carry on along the path.

Climbing again, bear left at a fenced area. The path now goes down into more dense woods. Once at the bottom cross the stream over a bridge, coming to a steep incline.

Carry straight on uphill, where a small path bears right. Almost at the top of the hill, turn left, along a wide path. Still climbing, follow this path round, as it bends.

Coming out on flat ground, you pass the cricket ground (C).

Cross over the road heading up the wide grass/mud path, passing through woods of Birch and Oak. As the path slowly climbs, admire the views across the valley.

Reaching the top, bear left, then turn right.

Grass path brings you back into Ridge car park.

Linton's car park is across the road.

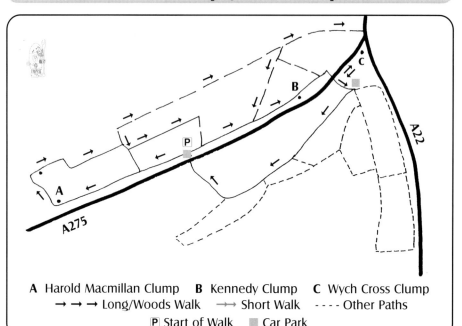

A Harold Macmillan Clump **B** Kennedy Clump **C** Wych Cross Clump
→ → → Long/Woods Walk →→ Short Walk - - - - Other Paths
P Start of Walk ■ Car Park

Access/Parking:	Churlwood car park (page 8)
Map reference:	EX 135. 417311
Distance:	2½ mls (Short walk). 3½ mls (Long walk).
Time:	1¼ hrs (Short walk). 2¼ hrs (Long walk).
Terrain:	Walk suitable for all. Wide grass paths. Muddy when wet. 2 slight hills. Long walk as short walk, going into woods, more slippery.
Refreshments:	Wych Cross Tea Rooms ½ ml.

Points of interest

A. Harold Macmillan Clump.
Harold Macmillan Clump was planted in memory of Harold Macmillan who lived nearby.

B. Kennedy Clump.
Kennedy Clump was planted in 1964 to commemorate the visit by John F. Kennedy, President of U.S.A. in the previous year.

C. Wych Cross Clump.
Wych Cross Clump was planted in the 1700's, but is not mentioned until the 1900's.

Open woodland. Great for exploring. Note variation details on the long walk.

Route directions

Leave the car park bearing left.

Path brings you out on to the main wide heather, grass/mud path. Bracken and gorse bushes are scattered each side. A Scots Pine wood looms on your right.

Carry on along the path.

Ignore the right junction.

Cross over a concrete road. Carry straight on.

Ignore the right turn. Carry straight on.

Path then veers right, downhill, passing around the first of the three magnificent Scots Pine clumps. Harold Macmillan Clump (A).

Carry on downhill.

Now a climb back up and around, bearing right, on a bracken/heather path to the recreation ground.

Follow the path around ground, past the car park, and out on to a wide grass path.

Path twists, then straightens as you wander between gorse bushes.

At the junction turn right. Note the path to the left going downhill into the woods*.

Climbing up on to flat ground. Turn left.

You are now back on the main path.

Once on the flat, with the woods on your left, the path leads back to the car park.

Carry on along the wide path, past the car park. You come to Kennedy Clump (B).

This area leaves you with a peculiar feeling of destiny as you move off towards Wych Cross Clump.

Stay on the path. When you reach the road, cross and turn left, carry on along the path to Wych Cross Clump (C).

Retrace your steps along the path until you come to the Reservoir car park.

Harold Macmillan Clump

65

Bear right on path passing by the Reservoir car park.

Carry on down the path, bearing right, at the junction.

Path comes out to a road. Cross over, the car park is opposite.

Long walk

A walk on the wildside, follow directions to turn point left down into woods (indicated*)

Now turn right. Walk along the path as it slowly climbs, beside fenced area.

Scots Pine, Oak and Holly create this wood of adventure.

Carry on along the path.

As the woods enlarge, dips and gullies emerge.

Variations to long walk

You can wander in and out of these gullies, absorbing the atmosphere of the area. It is a children's paradise.

Or you can walk along the side path, and look in on nature.

Follow the path right to the end, it takes you out onto the main road. Cross over, then turn right, walk along the grass verge, to the car park.

Or, near a fallen tree, there is a track leading up into the woods. Follow this track, through bracken undergrowth, and out on to the grass plain. Cross over the plain to the road* , visit Kennedy Clump (B).

*Or bear left once in the woods, and a tiny track leads out on to the road. Cross over. Follow the path ahead, then turn right.

All the variation walks come out to the Reservoir car park, carry on to Wych Cross Clump (C) then return by the same path to the Reservoir car park. Follow directions of the short walk back to the car park.

J. F. Kennedy Clump

Path down and up on Clumps Warren/Stream Walk

WALK 23   Millbrook/Nutley Travels

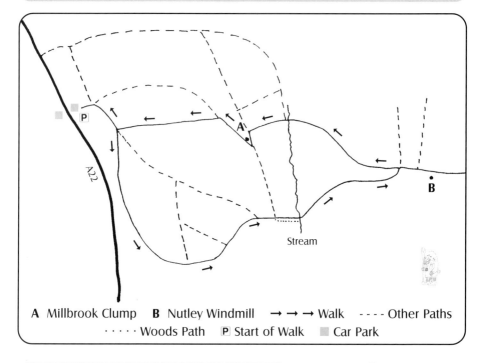

A Millbrook Clump   **B** Nutley Windmill   → → → Walk   - - - - Other Paths
· · · · · Woods Path   P Start of Walk   ▦ Car Park

Access/Parking:	Millbrook East car park (page 8)
Map reference:	EX 135. 440298
Distance:	4 mls (Short walk). Long walk can include Two Clumps and a Windmill (Walk 2), and Bushy Willow (Walk 3).
Time:	2 hrs (Short walk). 5-6 hrs (Long walk).
Terrain:	Short walk, wide paths. Muddy when wet. Steep hills. Long walk, see Walks 2, 3.
Refreshments:	Nutley village 2 mls. Ashdown Llama Centre 1 ml.

Points of interest

A. Millbrook Clump.

Millbrook Clump was one of the original clumps planted in 1825, although not mentioned in early details of the area.

B, C, are included in the long walk.

B. Nutley Windmill.

C. Friends' Clump.

Route directions

Short walk

Follow the path over the grass picnic area, to the back.

Go through a gate, turn right going downhill.

A wide mud path guides you through dense bracken and gorse as you see a sweeping landscape. Looking over the horizon is the path you are going to walk.

Carry on downhill. As the path winds, stay on it.

Coming to fencing, there are two paths ahead.

Both lead to the stream at the bottom.

Bear right.

You are heading into a wooded area. The path is more rugged, as you walk beside the fenced area.

Stay on the open rugged path, bearing left.

Once at the stream, stepping stones or a splash, are the way over.

Path leads up a steep hill, out of the woods, into the open again.

Follow the direction of the path, as it bears left.

Coming to a fenced area at the top of hill, bear left.

Look back over the valley just walked, see if you can spot a Sparrowhawk circling overhead.

Carry on up towards the woods, and stay on the path as it goes into Oak woods.

Gorse alley

Carry on along the path as it slowly changes from mud to grass and look out for a path to the right.

This path leads to Nutley Windmill (B).

Point B is where the Walks 2 and 3 continue on for the long walk.

Return to point B, and continue on short walk directions.

Retrace your steps through the woods, from the Windmill (B) back to the top of the hill bearing left.

Looking over the horizon, you can see Millbrook Clump (A) in the distance.

Bear left. Follow the wide path downhill.

Again gorse and bracken with an odd Scots Pine tree guide you down.

As the path bears right, you come to some Evergreens standing proud. Now bear left. A mud path brings you to the stream.

A small bridge keeps the feet dry, cross over and keep to the left as the path starts to climb.

Single Scots Pine trees dot the landscape as you make your way uphill on a sandy/mud path.

At the junction turn left. A short way along path, take the right junction heading straight uphill.

You come to Millbrook Clump (A).

As you pass by Millbrook Clump, making your way uphill, stay on the wide path to the junction.

Turn left. Path is still climbing. *Notice the corridor of gorse you are walking through. Smell the flowers. They have a distinct smell of coconut.*

Once at the top of the hill, turn right. You are now back on the path where the walk first started. Go back to the gate and across the picnic area to the car park.

Pathway near Friends' Clump

USEFUL TIPS / INFORMATION

Take a walking stick.
This comes in useful when crossing streams, wandering over open areas, or in deep woods.

Combination walks
Always check both walks for suitability and time scale before starting out.

O/S Explorer 135. Maps are not to scale. Walks are denoted by numbers on maps on pages 6, 7, 8 and 9.

Toilet/Refreshment areas. (In order)
A22 Ashdown Llama Centre.
A22 Wych Cross Tea Rooms.
A22 Nutley Village.
A22 William IV Pub. Full Meals. Snacks.
A275 Red Lion Pub. Bar Meals. Restaurant.
A26 Duddleswell Garden Centre.
A26 Duddleswell Tea Rooms.
B2188 Half Moon Inn. Hot/cold drinks, food.

The Ashdown Forest Centre.
Wych Cross, Forest Row, East Sussex RH18 5JP. Tel: 01342 823583
Opening times:
Weekdays 1st April-30th Sept. 2pm - 5pm.
Weekends/Bank Holidays 11am - 5pm.

S.B. Publications publish a wide range of local interest books and guides. For a free catalogue write to: S.B. Publications, 19 Grove Road, Seaford, East Sussex BN25 1TP